INSTAGRAM MARKETING

Brand New 2019 Guide to All-New Secret Strategies for Growing Your Brand and Generating Passive Income from Social Media

professional advice. The content within this book has been derived from various sources. Please consult a licensed professional before attempting any techniques outlined in this book.

By reading this document, the reader agrees that under no circumstances is the author responsible for any losses, direct or indirect, that are incurred as a result of the use of the information contained within this document, including, but not limited to, errors, omissions, or inaccuracies.

Table of Contents

Introduction

You're ready to begin your journey into the world of Instagram marketing, and you are not quite sure where you need to start. There are basic concepts that spread across all of the social media platforms that can help make your business effective.

Being present on social media shows both customers and clients alike that you are aware of what they want and need from the business. Being able to respond directly to customers or take polls to gain a better perspective on what they are looking for will help you build your company and online following as you begin posting more information about topics that your followers are interested in.

Customers prefer human interaction. They don't want to be force-fed a sales tactic, which is why social media is a clever way to promote your company and sales while still keeping the positive and face-friendly look overall. On top of that, social media is one of the fastest ways to spread the word. More people are turning to social media and internet opinion pages for reviews of companies in order to see what the quality of service is going to be like if they decide to choose them. Being present and aware of your online reputation is important for both your business and your clients. Customers don't want to work with a company that is associated with negative publicity, even if that negativity is not directed at the company itself.

Consider the BP oil spill back in 2010. Investors began pulling out quickly when it became clear that the situation was not going to be controlled. Negative publicity for your company, or one that is invested in you, could be your downfall unless it is handled efficiently and tactfully. Social media is a very effective tool to use in these situations. Not only do you have access to all of your followers, but those followers also have the ability to share your news and offer their comments and opinions with real-time updates. By being present online, you are able to respond quickly to them in order to help resolve any situations that may occur and prevent any future negative press from spreading.

Customer service is evolving rapidly to keep up with the way that people communicate and learn about new products and businesses. Using Instagram marketing is a great way to promote your company to others; the app allows for searches on topics through hashtags, and also allows you to determine what it is that customers are searching for in products.

As you develop your skills on the social media platforms, you'll notice a rise in your company profits and following. You will have more customers that begin sharing pictures of your products that they bought online and start tagging their posts with your brand name as they show off their new items. As others begin to follow your page and share your online information on their pages, you will notice your following grow even more. For every person that follows your account, your company will be able to stretch further onto different feeds. The Instagram algorithm works in favor of popular content creators that have a lot of followers, comments, likes, and regular postings on their pages. You don't need to overwhelm your followers' feeds with your company's business postings, however.

The goal of using social media for your business is to be able to better communicate with your customers, while also being able to advertise and market to others without having to spend a ridiculous sum of money. The Internet is a prominent form of communication and a large shopping network. It's the perfect time to begin spreading information about your business and providing tips and advice in order to intrigue people and draw them into visiting and liking your page. Instagram is one of the largest social media bases that has grown from a picture-posting app to a business-to-business and business-to-customer app. Advertisements with direct links to websites have been made to fit perfectly onto the newsfeed as you are scrolling through your posts. More people are going to be looking to buy something from an Instagram influencer, product advertisement, or even through a search using hashtags to find the product. Get involved in that market and your following will begin to grow rapidly.

Even if you don't know where to start, you know that having a social media account is a top priority in order to grow your business. Through reading this book, you will learn how social media can help you build your business and increase sales by gaining followers and raising overall brand awareness along the way. You'll learn how to engage your customers and sell your product, all through one thread of communication.

There is a science behind the success stories of businesses on social media, and now you can be one of those success stories, too. It is time to get involved in the future of social media marketing.

Chapter 1: What Social Media Can Do for Your Business

Social media is a rapidly growing arena for everything from the posting of videos to car sales, so it should come as no surprise that big business is growing on there, too. However, what can it actually do to help grow your business?

Before selling any product, you have to get your name out there and spread the word of your new social media presence. By adding links to your social media accounts on your company website, you are encouraging people to follow you online in order to get the most up to date information as soon as you release it. When you put your company website on your social media profile, it gives your clients a way to go directly to your website. This will allow your customers to contact your company for more information, and it is more likely to create online buyers.

Social media is the main way that companies are beginning to show involvement with their customers and community by promoting events they are sponsoring or releasing news to their clients. Real-time communication has become extremely important for customer satisfaction in today's businesses. People don't want to wait for answers to their questions or for help resolving any issue they might have. With social media, people have direct access to comments and post feedback for companies, making any kind of wait-time for results obsolete.

Press releases are a thing of the past and take more time to be processed out to customers. By using social media, your company is able to deliver news and updates to clients in real time, while also allowing them to share the news with others and encouraging a faster spread of communication. By letting customers share your company's posts and information, it also allows new people to follow your company page and learn more about your business.

Businesses are turning to Instagram and Facebook, among other social media platforms, to better communicate with their customers and spread the word about their business and future plans. To go about doing this, companies first have to understand the best ways to create brand awareness online and how to draw in new followers.

Building a successful online following will take time. However, there are techniques and skills that will help you build an online following and create a popular social media site, while still promoting your business and keeping in contact with your customers.

The Basics of Brand Awareness

Building brand awareness isn't going to happen overnight, and it won't come from pushing online sales and marketing campaigns on people you don't know. Most of the time, brand awareness actually comes from the process of developing relationships with your customers. Most customers seek an interpersonal relationship with companies from which they plan to purchase.

Think about it in terms of buying a car. If you walk into a car dealership and the salesperson acts aloof while giving you a cut-and-dried spiel about the car, you might feel like the personal aspect of the exchange is a little closed off. However, if the representative you're working with is friendly and shares stories with you, you feel a connection with that person and begin developing trust in them and in the company. Social media essentially works the same way when it comes to brand awareness. You don't have to constantly post about the company and what is happening, but you could post something that your customers relate to, or share something funny to help lighten the mood and develop trust with your customers. Building a relationship with a company is one of the biggest aspects when it comes to return customers. More often than not, people that feel welcomed in a place of business, instead of targeted by sales associates, are going to return for that same experience again. It's human nature to dislike being targeted when it comes to sales. It's frustrating and annoying to have people popping up all around you and trying to force products on you when you aren't even shopping for those items.

How do you effectively get around that issue but still market to your customers? You want to create advertisements that are fun and easygoing. While they do capture the attention of Instagram users, it won't feel like a sales tactics is being shoved down their throats. It gives them the option to scroll past the ad or click to learn more. The Instagram algorithm, which we will review later, notes how long someone looks at a post. So, when you have more people looking at your advertisements and social media posts, it creates more of the same type of post on their page to hold their attention for longer. More attention per post is the main goal of the Instagram algorithm, and shoppers work to its advantage.

Social media has become such a prominent part of a business that over 50% of brand awareness comes from the company's online sociability. What does it mean to have brand awareness, and how can you go about building up your popularity?

Brand awareness comes down to how well your business can be recognized. Another word that you could connect to awareness is reputation. While you are building your business, you want to develop a positive relationship with your clients early on and build up your reputation with customers as much as possible. Social media can almost be considered the same thing as word of mouth nowadays due to how it facilitates the spread of information and the ability to share opinions online.

In order to create more brand awareness, you should use recognizable hashtags. Hashtags can be clicked on and followed through social media in order to see all the posts on the platform with that hashtag attached. Imagine trying to find a company that works on different online marketing strategies. Customers could go on Instagram and search #marketing. Any pictures attached to that hashtag would come up, and if your company has been tagging its posts with that simple word, you could end up bringing new people to your page.

A new tactic on Instagram is its story mode. Accounts can post videos or pictures to their online story and it only keeps it up there for 24 hours. A story post will notify any of your followers that you have posted to your story so that they know to go look at it. Instagram is more photo-based than any other social media platform, so if you want to post videos as well, it's best to keep them short. Videos have the capability to share more information at a faster rate. It makes the time that a user is watching more valuable, and, typically, more information can be provided in the same amount of time used to stop and read a caption. So, if people are scrolling through their feeds and a video starts playing, they might stop to see what it's about.

You're not playing a movie; just give your followers a taste of what you're trying to show. By not giving them the entire picture upfront, they are going to want to come to your page in order to get more information about the product or service that you are selling. Big business companies like Apple and Microsoft never even say their company name in any commercial. Why? People know their products and their company. You want to be able to build your company up online to where, when people see your logo, they instantly know the company that is writing that message. Brand awareness also comes with brand trust, which leads to people buying your product and you gaining a following. In order to get more people to follow your page and like your photos, interaction is key. The more you interact with people following your account, the more you are going to build the following that you need.

Gaining Followers Online

In order to get your business out there on social media, you are going to want people to share your post to their page as gain more attraction to your business page. In order for people to share your posts, however, you are going to need to build a following on your page first.

There have been several studies done on social media marketing to see how popularity works on the web. There are certain styles of pictures and promotion tactics that followers are drawn to more than others. However, the main way to get new followers and attract attention to your page is through hashtags. While there is a limited number of hashtags that can be added to each photo, 30 to be exact, research shows that, ideally, you want to have anywhere from 8 to 10 hashtags attached to the post. Overwhelming your post with an assortment of hashtags will not only be distracting for the customer viewing the post, but will also make your business appear tacky and unorganized. You shouldn't need to post any more than 10 in order to get your main points across.

Hashtags are meant to be used as filters to allow users to find more relatable and interesting content. They are also used to make online connections from photos to businesses and people alike in order to connect them through similarities. Two entirely different people could post pictures with #sixflags on them, but they can connect through sharing similar experiences with the rest of the world while also marketing the excitement and enjoyment that Six Flags can provide.

When people are able to connect with one another based on similar experiences and desires, it creates a web of communication that the Internet hub has been building for years. Instagram used to be a social outlet only and wasn't originally designed to be a shopping platform for internet marketers. Nowadays, people have instant access to everything and are able to review companies and their standard of care for customers within a few short clicks. Building a following online is the best way to prevent people from searching for negative aspects of your company. By providing excellent customer service and online assistance to people through the different social media platforms, you will create a positive spike in the algorithm data. Your customers will continue to follow and promote you through commenting on and sharing your posts.

What type of hashtags should you be adding to your social posts? According to Ana Gotter, writer for the Shopify Blogs, there are six categories of hashtags that people are looking at and that you should focus on for your posts:

1. **Branded Hashtags** — First, you have your branded hashtags, which are used to promote your company name. You should use these on most of your posts, especially when posting specifically about something that your company is doing. It creates brand recognition, and whenever someone uses your product or attends an event for your company, you should encourage them to use the hashtag as well. This will help spread brand awareness and give your company the opportunity to reach a broader spectrum of followers.

2. **Contest Hashtags** — Next, you have contest hashtags, which are rather easy to understand. They are used to promote any contests or promotional giveaways that your company

sponsors. You can pair these easily with the name of your company to create a gateway for followers to get to your page for more information.

3. **General Hashtags** — General hashtags are the most diverse and hit the widest spread of audience. Sometimes, they even include the name of the social media site they are on, creating internal marketing for the site itself. For example, general hashtags can range anywhere from #petsofinstagram to #ilovemyjob. The generality of the topic allows people to post from all different categories and still fall under that hashtag, as well as find similar posts and photos that draw their interest.

4. **Niche-Specific Hashtags** — Niche-specific hashtags revolve around a specific topic. You will often see these on things such as products designed after pop culture. You might see advertisements for things like *Doctor Who* products designed after the hit TV show, or *Harry Potter* or *The Hobbit* jewelry or accessories that are replicas or similar to

designs from the movies. When people look at the hashtags #doctorwho or #harrypotter and find a product related to the topic of interest, they will more than likely consider buying it.

5. **Timely Hashtags** — Timely hashtags have to do with the "now" topics and usually incorporate holidays or special events that are going on. You might have hashtags like #valentines2019 or #christmasvacation, or even smaller holidays such as #nationalbestfriendday, which may be a trending topic for that moment.

6. **Entertaining Hashtags** — The entertaining hashtags are usually things like #toobadsosad or #overit which are more attention-grabbing and funnier. Usually, they are somewhat relevant to the topic, but might not be directly related. Using #overit could be on a post about a stressful work day and being ready to go to bed and start fresh the next day. Even though the post itself doesn't specifically say anything about being "over it," the topic and statement both align with the post.

You should pick out a series of hashtags that best sums up your post and pictures in order to keep things fresh. You should also avoid using the exact same hashtags for every single post. You want to be able to diversify your posts in order to reach different people online and have a wider span of people learning about your company and your promotions. The only hashtag that you should use every time is your branded hashtag, and even then, you should only use it on posts promoting your business. If you are sharing someone else's post or another company post, give them credit by adding their hashtag and commenting on either what they are doing or what you hope to accomplish together.

When you use hashtags, you are able to look at what other people have posted associated with those hashtags as well. You should take note of the other hashtags they use on their posts so that you can add them to your list of potential ones to use in the future, or to research and see what people are saying on the topic. For example, while you may have used #marketing, you might notice that, on another user's post, they used #marketing and #publicrelations. You can then look into the hashtag for public relations and see where that takes you. You want to keep your business in the same category as what you are posting about, and you don't want to use random tags just to bring attention to the post. This will appear unprofessional and distasteful in the eyes of other business professionals who are looking at your posts.

Hashtags are a great way to find new topics for discussion as well. For example, if your business is all about marketing, you may have never thought about advertising for public relations. Being able to expand into different markets is much easier with social media because it creates connections through millions of different people across a multitude of topics.

Then, you have the Instagram storyboard. At one point you were only able to put up one story, all in a single cycle, for people to watch through. However, now there is a way that you can actually make multiple different stories for different categories and attach them to your profile. Instagram decided to call these new stories "highlights," and the platform allows them to stay on your profile for longer than the original 24 hours. Posting highlights creates a way for your followers to watch certain videos without having to view all of them. Let's say your company is having a company retreat and you want to create a story just for that specific day. You can title it "2019 Retreat" and then post only stories involving that retreat's activities and experiences for people to watch. They won't have to filter through any other story highlight information you have posted if it isn't relevant to what they're looking for.

So, now that you have built your page and developed a line of hashtags that work best for your brand, it's time to move on to creating your marketing campaign to get people to your website and buying your products. Make sure you are following other people in the industry to see what they are posting or what promotional activities they are running in order to get a better idea of how you can improve your own company's social media presence. It's a common misconception that watching your rival companies is cheating. Think about how often cell phone companies play cat and mouse with one another over the newest trends and technology: bigger screens, better headphones, more wireless capabilities. By watching what other companies do, you are able to hone in what people are expecting to get from the business. You can create your own version of the plan that other companies are developing because, at the end of the day, customers will choose the one that gives them the most positive feeling. Plus, it's good to be cordial with competing companies. Beyond it being a decent thing to do, friendly competition is a great way to get people interested in what's happening online.

For example, think back to when Wendy's and McDonald's had online Twitter comments going back and forth. It took the internet by storm and was reposted all over the different social media platforms. People were sharing and talking about it, which encouraged other companies to get involved online in the clapback marketing comments. All of the competition was promoting their food items, and talking about the cooking styles of the fast food restaurants and the deals they had going on. While it was funny and attention-grabbing, people were also spreading the word that the chicken nuggets at Wendy's were more expensive but fresher than those at McDonald's. Your competition isn't your enemy, and it could be good to use some of their strategies.

Following your opposing companies also allows you to see what types of marketing strategies they use to bring in their customers. This can help you develop your plans to be more effective in the future. As people use different businesses, they are going to like certain aspects about one and other things about another. The more research that you conduct as you study up on customers that search through similar hashtags, the more you will notice a trend in the types of business styles they like and the environment they are looking for when they choose a business to work with. This allows you to add to and change your marketing strategy to suit more people's wants when it comes to picking a company.

You can search through different hashtags on Instagram, which allows you to find content that is related to what you are trying to post. It could help you find inspiration on what to post while also allowing you to see what others are currently talking about in the market, or what they are looking to achieve from the market. You may also find other businesses that you can work with, depending on the hashtags that they have attached to their post.

By following different companies and individuals, you are getting a better assessment of what is going on in the industry, and how to use it to your advantage when you begin a new marketing campaign. Gaining followers isn't an overnight project, nor is it a one-time effort. Your company should constantly be striving to increase its online following on all social media platforms by encouraging followers of one platform to like and follow you on the other platforms as well. If you have Instagram followers who haven't liked your Facebook page yet, then you now have the opportunity to gain followers on that platform as well.

Followers begin to like and comment based on the content of the posts, but they can always search through hashtags to find your company. When you begin posting regularly, make sure you include different types of engaging posts for them to read and think about. Otherwise, they might unfollow you to stop clogging their feed. Make sure your posts are relevant to your followers and the projects they are working on or looking to begin on in the near future. For example, if you see a company looking to expand into a new market, you can send them a message online and get on their radar early. You might not get anywhere with it right away, but by being in the background and following them online as they develop the marketing side of their business further, you can continue to offer help along the way in order to keep their mind drawn back to your company if they need assistance. Build your network in any way you can. You probably won't know all your followers, but interacting with them and showing interest in the things that they do will help make your page successful online.

Chapter 2: Creating an Effective Marketing Strategy

Pages very rarely become popular by accident. You might hear the one in a million story about the person who posted a picture online and it blew up and made them famous instantly, but, more than likely, your popular pages started with a plan of action. Just posting information on your social media isn't going to draw people to your page. In order to gain followers, you have to provide content that they want to look at. People on Instagram are looking through post after post as they scroll through their feed of followers. If they go to the search homepage, they see randomly generated photos that they may find interesting based on what they have liked in the past and currently follow. This is because an algorithm notices when you look at something for a longer period of time than you spend on other posts. When you look at something for an extended period of time, the Instagram algorithm studies that topic and pushes out more information related to that in order to keep your attention on their platform for longer. Social media sites are not making money if you aren't using the platform. Companies are paying them to advertise their content to users in order to build up their reputation in the process. The longer you look at something, the more advertisements get thrown on the feed, which creates more profit for the advertising company and the social media platform itself. That's why you need to know how to use the algorithm to your advantage when you begin posting regularly online and communicating with your followers.

On the Instagram search page, you'll notice a few different things: the search bar at the top, the clickable category choices, and the photos and videos on display. You have the choice to either look through the photos selected for you based on what you've liked and the different profiles you follow, or you can click on a topic bar at the top and look through the photos that appear under that specific topic. If you're looking for a specific hashtag, you can always type that into the search bar as well in order to find pictures with that same label. People usually search for general hashtags, which is why it's a good idea to have different categories of tags on your post to increase the likelihood that someone will come across it and look at it.

There are several ways to draw the attention of viewers in order to get them to follow your page or like a photo that you posted. There are a lot of techniques that will help you get to the base you want, and they also help you sell your product. Let's say you're trying to raise money for a charity event and you want to get more people than just your followers involved. You have to come up with a way to spread the word while maintaining the hype. You could make a contest to get the word spread from person to person by having people compete by tagging one another online. You could also ask followers to donate a dollar for a special promotional rate. Whatever it is you are trying to achieve online, developing a strategy is your first step.

The Posting Algorithm

The posting algorithm is a mathematical magic formula in a computer that recognizes how popular posts are and who likes them based on how many times they have been looked at and how long someone looks at them. The more that people look at a post about a certain topic, the more likely it is that the algorithm will put more of that content in their news feeds for them to view. It gives Instagram the views and time that they want on their platform while the person gets new posts to view on a favorite topic.

The main idea of any social media site is to consistently post relevant content for your followers. If you are not posting consistently and the information is not updated, people might lose interest in your page. Each post is accounted for in the Instagram algorithm, which means that the more you post, the more likely people are to see that content. If someone spends a longer period of time looking at one post over the others, then the algorithm likes it more and deems it more credible than other posts. The more credible your posts are, the more likely it is that your company's posts will appear at the top of content.

Think about it like this, if you post a team office photo and everyone in that photo likes it, the algorithm will note the popularity and extend it to your next post as well, under the assumption that it will have the same popularity levels. The more posts you make, the more the algorithm can average out the popularity. While not all posts will get hundreds of likes, you can attempt to make them as compelling as possible by running a contest or running promotions for liked content.

The algorithm, in particular, is looking for people to stay on and use Instagram. The longer they are looking at their feed online, the more opportunities it creates to show them advertisements for products and companies, which is how Instagram makes its money. So, if your posts are capable of capturing peoples' attention for an extended period of time, then Instagram is going to reward that by pushing it higher in the algorithm of what posts are seen.

How do you make the algorithm work in your favor? There are several ways to get your information to the top of your followers' feed. While Instagram was originally designed for users to post photos, videos began gaining popularity as well. The Instagram algorithm does not prioritize videos unless the audience looking at them does. This means that, if your followers don't take the time to stop and watch a video in their feed, the system isn't going to continue to push more videos to the top. It is only going to prioritize what the user is looking at most frequently

(Cooper, 2019). Take videos into consideration by determining how long your followers are looking at them. While you don't want to have long drawn out videos, thirty seconds to a minute will hold their attention. Then, the algorithm notices them staying longer on your page and looking at your posts, pushing you further up on the viewing scale.

You also need to consider when to post. People aren't constantly looking at social media, but there are key times when people scroll through their feeds that should be noted. Depending on your audience, you may need to post in the early morning or late at night when you aren't awake. You can use planners like Instagram Scheduler or Hootsuite, which allow you to schedule posts for certain times and then automatically put them out when the system sends a signal. Using a scheduler also allows you the ability to plan posts in advance and schedule them to post at a later date. For example, if you are having a large company event and the flyers have already been made, you can take a photo of the flyer and schedule it to post a few days in advance of the event, along with other information released on the day of the event itself. You can even create a post with your event hashtag on it and set it up to release on the day of the event. This way, you don't have to worry about posting while everything else is being planned.

Another key aspect to take advantage of is simply asking people to turn on their notifications for your company's posts. When you think about it logically, the notification setting is probably one of the easiest ways to get your followers to look at your posts. When a notification pops up on your phone, you automatically go to see what it's about. Now that phones give you the ability to just click on the notification and follow it to the link or page, people have more ease of access to their social media and messages, and can look at them just as quickly as the notification that pops up.

Running a contest on Instagram is also a great way to boost yourself up in the algorithm. Usually, contests consist of tagging people in the post or following and posting something with a company hashtag attached. This creates an influx of followers and comments on posts that make your posts seem more popular in the system. While running contests is a quick way to boost your score in the system, it does average out, and you have to make sure that you keep your posting up to keep the algorithm from pushing you back down the ladder.

Overall, the algorithm breaks down into three categories: content, consistency, and attention. The more consistently you post, the more likely people will see your page and begin following you. The content needs to be well-timed, and message should be delivered using descriptive hashtags from different categories. Both of those combined get you the attention you need in order for people to view, like, and comment on your posts and photos. This may convert visitors into followers who can constantly see the content that you post.

Using Effective Photography

Photography has a lot to do with how a product is marketed. There are several factors that go into making a photo post-worthy and attention-grabbing. You don't need to have a fancy camera or a professional photographer to take a good photo. While it can be helpful to have someone take the photo for you, selfie pictures and candid moments can be some of the most emotion-filled photos because they represent the people behind the camera and what they are trying to voice for the company.

Good photography can make all the difference when it comes to people viewing your online profile. If the picture quality of your posts is consistently bad, then it will shed a bad light on the capabilities of a business. As ridiculous as it may seem, people are comparing the quality of your social media page to the work they believe that you can do for them. If you work for a marketing company and your Instagram page is just a host of blurry photos and non-descriptive posts, then customers might be less likely to trust your capability when it comes to producing clear and effective marketing projects.

A study done by Curalate in 2013 compiled four different aspects that had an effect on the popularity of a photo (Gotter, 2019):

- **Use Lighter Images** — While this may seem a little self-explanatory, having the correct lighting and colors in a photo can make a difference. No one wants to struggle to see the details of a photo. The details should be noticeable and bold to the eye.

- **More Background or White Space Is Preferred** — You don't want too much going on in a photo. If you are trying to sell a new boat, you shouldn't have a picture filled with different boats and yours in the middle. More than likely, you'll have the boat you are advertising on a plain or simple background so that the person's eye is drawn directly to the object that you are promoting.

- **Dominance Matters** — Just like having one item in the picture, it's best not to go color crazy. The study showed that if the more dominant color was blue rather than red, the photo produced more likes. This also held true for photos that only had one dominant color instead of many.

- **Use Contrasting Textures** — Having too many textures going on in your picture can be overwhelming, but having one or two to contrast with your dominant texture does bring attention to the photo.

Photography isn't the only attention-grabber on Instagram now. Quite a few marketing strategies have turned to quick and bold videos to push out to customers because they are more interactive and keep the customer looking at the product for longer than just a few seconds. A video is a little bit more complex to work with on social media in order to get the lighting and timing correct. You also don't want to have a long video that customers will stop watching halfway through. While videos can share more information with users, which, in turn, makes them more valuable, high-quality photos typically get an average of 36% more engagement. If you're going to use videos, keep them short. Instagram users are predominantly mobile users, and they aren't likely to stick around for more than ten to fifteen seconds at a time (Gotter, 2019).

When it comes to photos for Instagram, you should apply the same rules that you would to regular photography. You want to use natural lighting and the rule of thirds on your subject. Maybe even try shooting from different angles in order to get a more unique shot than any others you have posted before. You can always research the best photography techniques to use and get more guidelines on capturing the perfect shot. As long as you keep in mind the four main points listed above, you will be able to generate comments and likes on your posts.

Instagram Contest 101

An Instagram contest is one of the best ways to boost your following and get people to look at your page. It also gets people to come back and check for new information about the contest or results that they are waiting for. As we have previously established, the more that people look at your page, the more the algorithm likes your Instagram account. In order to run a successful contest on any platform, there are several steps you need to take before people start entering. While there are some legal steps that have to be taken with a contest, this book is only going to go over the basics of how to set the contest up and move it in the correct direction. You should discuss legal matters of the topic with your company lawyer.

1. **Contest Goal** — The first big step to planning any contest is figuring out your goal. Your goal isn't just to give away free stuff to internet strangers, so what exactly are you trying to achieve? Do you want to get more followers for your page? Are you just trying to get more likes and comments on some of your photos? Maybe you're trying to gauge the customer reaction to certain products or styles of work by having them vote on their favorites. Whatever you are trying to achieve needs to be your main goal, and you should write it down for data comparison later.

2. **Entry Method** — Next, you need to come up with the entry method. How do you want people to enter and participate in the contest? Do they need to like the photo and tag three friends? Do they need to post a separate picture with a particular hashtag for competition? Maybe they need to take a quick survey to be entered into the competition. However you plan to go about having people enter, make sure the instructions are clear. You should also develop a hashtag for the contest. Even if it's not necessary for people to create a new post with the hashtag, you want

something that people can click on and follow so that they can enter the contest as well. If you have people share the post as one of the requirements for the contest, it helps spread the word to different types of people and also helps your page as far as the algorithm is concerned.

3. **Contest Theme** — You also need to have a theme for the contest. Maybe it's winter time and you're running a contest to win new skis and a trip to the mountains. For obvious reasons, you would want to come up with something clever and catchy that relates the product to the competition. You could say something like #meanttoski and use it around Valentine's Day as a play on the phrase "meant to be." You are tying in the theme of falling in love with the new skis and the trip you are promoting. The idea for all themes remains the same. You want the theme to be clever but simple enough for people to remember it and share it with their friends and family.

4. **Pick a Winner** — Lastly, you have to decide when the cutoff date for the contest is and how to determine the winner. There are three ways

to pick a winner: random selection, selected jury, and popular vote. Random selection is a great way to pick from a large number of people. If all you asked them to do was like and follow your page, then it is easy enough to run their names through a random generator for a completely fair way to pick a winner. If you choose to have a jury judge the competition, then it involves a little more work. You'll need to bring in extra professionals to judge the submissions from all the competitors. While this is fair and is based on the quality of work rather than the randomness of a like and follow, it does take more time and attention to detail on the company's part. Finally, you have the voting method, which is simply having people vote to pick a winner. While this is a good way to get contestants motivated and followers involved, the scales can be tipped occasionally. If you have one contestant that has 10 followers while another has 10.5 million, the ability for that contestant to share their request for votes is higher than the other's. Is that necessarily a problem? No, but it does make it more of a popularity contest than a true competition. You can always use a mix of these methods as well. You could have judges narrow the contestants down to five and then allow followers to vote and pick their favorites. While there can still be a little bit of unfairness to the plan, it does narrow down the finalists to the people who actually successfully completed the competition.

After you are finished designing and finalizing all the contest work, you just have to promote it. Put the hashtag out there and advertise the contest on your different forms of social media for the company. Let people share it and spread the word as much as possible to get people motivated to join and participate in your company's main page.

When you go to announce the winner of the contest, make sure to thank people for participating. Again, it's all about the interaction you have on Instagram. You can also post when you will be holding another contest in order to keep people returning to your page to stay up to date with any promotion your company may be running.

Chapter 3: Influencer Marketing

Influencer marketing is a great way to get your company name and brand moving around the internet. While it may seem ridiculous to pay someone to promote your product through their social media, if you have someone with millions of followers wearing your products or talking about how much they enjoy working with your business, it's going to reach a broad spectrum of people.

You may be wondering how you could even go about getting an ambassador for your brand. Do you have to reach out to individuals? Do you know who the right person for your company would be? Where is the best place to start on the topic? The good news is that you really don't have to do any of that work. While you can go that route, it tends to be more challenging to get people to respond, and they might not necessarily be the right candidate to help you get your business going. There are several websites that can act as a middleman between you and the influencer. Those companies would have access to much more information about the individual, and you wouldn't have to worry about the ambassador's level of competence when it comes to the promotion of your brand. If they are working with a promotion company, then they know how to use their online presence to your company's advantage.

Instagram is one of the best platforms for utilizing influencer marketing. Instagram has around 800 million users every month. Facebook has a larger user base than Instagram, but Instagram users tend to be more engaged online. It is more effective for marketers to use Instagram because it has the highest interaction rate compared to all other social media platforms. Interaction between companies and customers makes it easier for shoppers to convert to customers. More users are interactive on the Instagram platform, which is why they don't tend to mind when influencers are promoting products. It has been documented that 65% of the top-performing posts include advertised products. It's a win-win for the parties on either side of the advertising.

Using influencers to market your products can be very profitable if done correctly. You have to make sure that you are using the right person who is in a similar niche as the items you are trying to promote. If the influencer already has a following that trusts what they are saying about the product, then you already have a foot in the door when it comes to closing the sale. You might want to continue to work with the same influencer over time to market different products. Once you have developed a good business relationship with them, it can benefit both the influencer and your business to continue promotions together. As people watch someone online and try and recreate looks or find products that they recommend, they tend to stick with the same person. They usually like the product, and it creates a connection between the influencer and the viewer; perhaps they like the same things, or the viewer likes the influencer's personality. Thus, they will continue to watch their videos and share the content which features your product.

Using Ambassadors to Build Your Brand

Like any marketing campaign, when you begin using a new resource, it's important to set goals for what you're looking to accomplish. Your goals need to be measurable. For instance, if you start running promotions through an ambassador program, then you should create a discount code using their name as a special ID; this way, you know whether people are coming to the website due to the ambassador's advertising or not. It also makes it easier for you to determine the benefit of using a particular Instagram influencer. If the product promotion doesn't seem to be working after a period of time, you might want to rethink your strategy. Come up with a new advertisement plan using that influencer, or switch influencers to try and reach a more receptive group of people.

When you begin looking for influencers, if you decide not to use a company middleman, then you need to look at the different aspects of what that influencer does. You need to know what the influencer's niche is. What is it that they specialize in talking about, and what are most of their posts and videos about? If you are a food marketer, then you might want to try and find a food blogger to talk about your work. You'll also want to study their reach. How many followers do they have? How many average likes and reposts do their posts have? If there aren't many people looking at their page or commenting on their work, then it isn't going to be doing your company a lot of good to use them for advertisement.

Another thing to notice is their voice. The way a person speaks or writes says a lot about them. Do they write passionately about the products they have, or are they just reading off of a script and giving you the basics? You want someone who is energetic to promote you; their enthusiasm will spread to other people and encourage them to seek out your product because the influencer was so excited to share that information with them. Their voice can still be professional and sell a big-ticket product if they know how to advertise correctly.

Next, you'll want to look into their engagement rate. Instagrammers like engagement. It's a more active form of social media, and with so many different capabilities from live videos to stories, it's important that the influencer is engaging with their followers. There are online calculators you can use in order to get the minimum amount of interaction an influencer should be using on their page in order to achieve the results that you are looking for.

Once you choose your influencer, it's time to set up a plan on how you want to achieve your goals. Again, there are some legal aspects that go into this section of the work that you have to be cautious of because it does come down to usage rights and payment for services. All of those should be discussed with a company HR representative or lawyer prior to signing an agreement.

The Influencer Marketing Hub says that these five things are the most crucial to getting your influencer to work for you ("The Beginner's Guide to Influencer Marketing", 2018):

1. **Set a Time Frame** — Create a reasonable time frame. You don't want the production to take too long, but you also don't want a rushed video when you are paying for promotion. It might be helpful for them to have check-in points, like when they complete the rough draft, so you can give them the time to make any edits before posting.

2. **Content Production** — How do you want the influencer to promote the product? Do you want them to use the product in a video? Do

you want to have them display it and talk about it and the benefits? Make sure you give the influencer clear instructions on how you want them to make the photo or video to best promote the product.

3. **Content Usage** — When it comes to content usage you need to think in advance about what else you may want to use this advertisement for. If you want to use it on other platforms, then you'll want full usage rights. This is something you'll want to discuss with your business and include in the contract for the influencer to sign as well.

4. **Compensation** — There are different ways you can pay an influencer, and it should be discussed and finalized before you begin working together. You could either pay them based on their performance and the results of the campaign, or you could pay them a flat fee per post that they do for your company. Whichever way you decide to do it, make sure to lay it all out in a finalized contract before starting.

5. **FTC Regulations** — As far as FTC (Federal Trade Commission) regulations go, your

influencer has to disclose that they are being sponsored by your company when they give the product review. For the security of the influencer and the company, it's important to know the full outline of the regulations to make sure that you are following any and all rules that are incorporated.

Influencer marketing is a great way to get the message about your product or company out. If you're just starting up on a new campaign, or even trying to get more followers and likes on your personal Instagram account, having someone help build your company's reputation is definitely going to help. While new followers may not know much about your company at first, influencers are definitely capable of swaying the public into a simple click to follow a page. They can be a great way for people to learn about your company and products, even in passing. They might be scrolling past your posts on their news feed at first, but then they will see the posts pop up. It all ties together with what you post as well. If your company is posting interesting or exciting photos and videos with dominant and eye-capturing shots, then your followers will stop to read and view those posts.

Chapter 4: Why Instagram Is Important for Employers

You may have some questions at this point. Why go through all this effort to post a few times on social media? Is it actually going to help my business, or am I just wasting my time? You have to keep in mind that, while social media has a lot of people floating around and a lot of big-time users, it takes time to build a following. Gaining followers isn't an overnight process, but if you continue to promote your profile, it will make your business more profitable.

Over 90% of marketers believe that social media marketing efforts increased their online visibility and communication between their business and social media users. It takes more time than traditional marketing does, but it is less stressful and can increase profitability. Brand awareness is going to be your greatest advantage when it comes to social media marketing. We have already discussed some techniques you can use to increase brand awareness for your company, but these techniques can also save you money when it comes to advertisement. For the most part, Instagram is free. You might be using some paid applications for post schedulers or paying a social media specialist to personalize your posts, but mostly it's a quick and easy way to talk about your brand and business without spending a ton of money. However, your company has the option to pay for online advertisements on different social media feeds and it will create pop-ups on different users' feeds. This will help them get to your website, and hopefully they will be following your social media as well once they have interacted on your company homepage. Instagram's formatting creates great opportunities for ecommerce businesses that are looking to break into social media marketing. If they want to use photos, videos, or the Instagram story ability, they can in order to attract more customers to their page. The visual concepts allow for businesses to market by showing off their actual products and displaying them in a modern way online. It's also a great way to keep your customers engaged and satisfied with your business. It's easy to review any comments and complaints and handle them effectively. Being able to interact with your company's customers will keep them happy. People like to have a voice, and when they see that a company is responding to their concerns, it keeps their satisfaction up. When customers see your company posting on social media, especially when replying to their queries and posting original content, it helps them build a positive image of your company in their minds. Regularly interacting with your customers proves that you and your business care about them. Once you get a few satisfied customers who are vocal about their positive purchase experiences, you can let the advertising be done for you by genuine customers who appreciate your products or services.

The other half of social media is SEO and conversions. Sharing content on social media gives users more reason to click through your website. The more quality content you share on your social media account, the more influx of website traffic you should see. As people read the information you put out in your posts, they will be more likely to continue on and visit your website. SEO requirements have changed from what they used to be. It used to be enough to just post on your company blog and make sure that your website and online newsletters were up to date. However, the Internet is looking at a lot more now. The more presence that you have on social media the better. Posting online creates consistency and validates your company's online presence. It also allows customers to click directly through to your website. You should have your company website posted on your profile page. Having direct access to a website allows people to avoid having to run through a search engine and see other options that pop up. By allowing people direct access to your website from your social media, you open yourself up to the opportunity to have more conversions for your company.

The more comfortable your business becomes with using Instagram and other social media platforms, the more productive you will become. Online businesses are becoming more popular every day. The fact of the matter is, the less that people have to shop around, the better it is for them. Being able to give your customers what they are looking for up front and supplying them with the option to avoid looking into other businesses is a way to create an immediate conversion. You want your followers to promote your company name and buy products from your business alone. Search engines have allowed people to find a huge variety of companies by what they are searching for. Now, social media has developed the same capabilities. It's the perfect place to build your company's reputation and promote sales from your page.

Building Sales Through Social Media

The entire point of marketing is to bring in sales. At the end of the day, your goal is to make that conversion from a viewer to a buyer. The first thing you need to do to make sales is to be present on the same platform that your customers are on. If you are looking for a young adult to adult market, then Instagram is the place to be. LinkedIn is more business-based and can be useful if you're looking to sell to other businesses. If you want to avoid some hassle, find the right market before you begin advertising your products. There are websites like Keyhole that can help you determine the age market that you are looking for.

Next, you have your influencers. Influencers make selling things easier because their followers are tuned into their market. You can also give your influencers a promo code which helps you track the effectiveness of their advertisements, but also promotes your business and gives people a discount for buying your product at the same time. For example, a lot of makeup business will use beauty bloggers to promote their products and, in turn, give them a promo code to sell the product at a discount of around 10-15% off. As a result, people will return to the beauty blogger for discounts on products, and it allows customers to buy the products at a lower rate. You get the benefit of a sale while the blogger gets a follower.

Brand advocates are also a great way to help promote your business. Brand advocates are a little different than influencers because they might not be popular on social media. However, they know your product and they like using it. Brand advocates are the way to go if you don't want to use an influencer. Real people can be enticed to promote products for you through their social media by being offered free products or discounts on items. Offering free stuff is a great way to get into anyone's good graces, especially if those items are usually on the more expensive side. This is how jewelry companies and makeup companies make some good investments by utilizing bloggers and influencers. The cost of a product is usually cheaper than paying someone to promote your business. The best part about brand advocates is that they already like your business. You're giving them a product that they already like, and they have already posted that they like your brand. You can then use this relationship to your advantage. The best way to sell something is to not have to say a word. Think about it like this: if you are shopping for an engagement ring, you're going to visit multiple stores, and the associates are going to try to upsell you on warranties and other products. You might feel like you are being overwhelmed by information. Hearing positive reviews from other people, though, will help you feel more comfortable. You want a company to care about you and the product they are selling, so hearing from someone else that they trust this brand and the company's work will go a long way in the eyes of other customers.

Another great way to involve customers in the sale experience is to promote their content. A great example is Coca-Cola. When you tag them in a post on Instagram, they often reply to your comment or picture, which increases the product experience for that person. When a company shares someone else's post, even if it does feature their product, they are showing the proof that people like this product. You can also drive more sales through social media by encouraging your customers to share their photos online. Be sure to take the extra step and share these user-generated photos on your own social media profiles. This is an easy way to increase loyalty with your existing customers, and it adds credibility to your brand whenever potential customers visit your social media profiles (Barker, 2018). Creating a brand hashtag not only increases brand awareness; it also allows your followers and product users to share their brand experiences with others. When you see the posts and photos that you are tagged in, you have the opportunity to respond and comment on their photos, increasing your interaction rating in the algorithm.

Remember, you want your company page to be as popular as possible with more followers, likes, and comments in order for the algorithm to push you into the trend pages and promote your company's

Instagram. So, even when you are simply sharing your followers' tagged posts, you are still increasing your overall rating in the algorithm due to your activeness on the platform.

Your Instagram posts should also teach your customers about your business. This comes back to the idea that your posts should encourage your customers and clients to follow your page to your company website. By providing how-to content in your posts, you will be providing customers with the information that will inspire them to try your product and see what all the rage is about. Other companies will be drawn to your page if you post tips and advice on how to improve on your business and how to market products. Not everything has to be business on the platform, and sending friendly well wishes to your customers around the holidays is pretty typical as well. However, in order for people to know what your company is doing and for you to promote your business products, your posts should consist of techniques or strategies that your company is using, or quick video clips of a specific product being used. Think about how car commercials work when you want to get an idea of how to draw people in.

Sometimes, these commercials only show a small part of the car, like the wheels spinning or the headlights turning on, and it's just enough to get you to imagine the whole picture and the capabilities that this sleek new car could have. It makes you want to look into that product even more. The teasers of a good product are enough to turn people's heads.

The Future in Internet Marketing

If you're still not convinced that internet marketing and social media platforms are the way to go, then you need to think about the future. Online marketing has already become very dominant on the scene, but by the time the year 2020 comes around, more and more people will be using their mobile phones and handheld tablets to do the majority of their shopping. When physical printing becomes obsolete, the online market will be the only thing left.

Now is the time to be perfecting your skills in internet marketing, especially in the realm of social media. Over the next few years, Generation Z will be growing up, and they will become the major consumers of the era. Since this generation grew up surrounded by technology, they were raised with YouTube videos and smartphones instead of TV advertisements and magazines. They have entirely different priorities than the generations before them, but they also have a different way of looking at life. Due to the fact that they are raised with technology, they never have to wait for much and have instant access to whatever they need, including buying things online. Generation Z is referred to as having an 8-second filter, which they use to find content that they care about and actually want to look at. They don't have to waste any time scrolling through loads of information when they can just bypass it by finding exactly what they want.

Companies are now having to figure out how to capture the attention of this generation and keep them focused on the product being sold within an 8 second time frame before they move on. If they can't capture their attention and hold it, the sale will be bypassed and they will move on to the next segment of their news feeds. However, it isn't just this generation that is turning to technology for shopping. More and more businesses are closing their physical doors due to online shoppers. Warehouses are limitless in terms of the internet, and people don't have to wait in line to get what they want. Shopping online has become as easy as clicking three buttons and tapping the screen to pay for something online. With the age of online shopping on the rise, marketers need to be prepared to keep up.

In order for companies to stay profitable in a constantly changing technological world, they need to be able to focus on the trending topics and platforms of that moment. Advertising on Facebook used to make major waves because that was the platform where most people were looking and making friends. You could follow company pages and that would be enough. However, now Instagram has become the most popular social media platform for people; it offers a wide variety of photo and filter options, story abilities, and other features that the other social media platforms don't have. By advertising and building marketing strategies for Instagram, there is the option to create a quick and easy link directly to the company website that's posting the ad. The posts also don't stand out as ads right away, but look similar to any other Instagram post until you notice the "swipe up" banner at the bottom that will take you to the shopping site.

The Internet is the future of all resources. Marketing is becoming entirely digital and is moving away from physical print due to the fact that fewer people are buying anything physically printed. With practically everyone online in the social media world, selling a product has never been easier. Instagram users are not only more engaged, but they are also usually online shoppers. A study recently showed that 72% of Instagram users made a purchase decision after seeing something advertised on Instagram. The most common categories that saw sales were clothing, makeup, shoes, and jewelry. Instagram shoppers are easy to convert when it comes to sales because they know what they are looking for in products. They are following the brands they like, and as they discover new trends in their newsfeed, they continue to buy new products that suit them. That's why Instagram is so high on the charts for influencer marketing. People are following beauty bloggers and trend setters that have unique styles because they want to be on the same path as they follow their brand ambassadors' advice on what to buy and what to wear.

Internet marketing has become more prominent in recent years due to the fact that people are buying more products online than they are from physical stores. Through social media, and Instagram in particular, it's becoming easier to go from advertisement to webpage with the swipe of a finger. There are different banners that can be displayed on advertisements, including ones that say "Learn More" or "Shop Now" at the bottom of the picture. These allow you to simply swipe the line upward, and it will automatically load the business website for you from the advertisement you were looking at.

Chapter 5: The Pros and Cons of Internet Marketing

Social media has been criticized from day one of its existence and there are certainly some downsides that come with it. That's not the question that you should be worrying about, though. With every negative there comes the opportunity for growth and development, so while the list below may be considered as cons or negatives in the eyes of some, it might be of little concern to others.

Internet marketing definitely has its pros and cons, and depending on how you look at it, some issues can be representative of both sides. Social media is constantly running, and this gives people the prime opportunity to make the internet work for them. There are ways to work around and overcome each problem with positivity and make it work for you as you develop your business strategy. However, you still have to be prepared to deal with the issues as they arise, and any negative effects that online marketing could bring your company.

Online marketing and sales go hand in hand in the

social media world. Marketing strategies are put to the test as they display advertisements in different places on customers news feeds, along with posting sales and promotion tactics to their company's social media pages, as well. People don't tend to notice that they are being sold something when they look at fun advertisements and see people like celebrities or other key influencers holding a product or using certain items in videos. In the subconscious mind, it does take root and can be effective as far as sales go, but it's hard to produce concrete results when social media sales aren't recorded in any concrete way.

The Pros and Cons

Let's start with the pros of social media marketing. The number one pro across most business boards is that social media marketing is effective and cost-efficient. Companies don't have to spend a fortune on advertisements anymore because social media is allowing them to put out constant messages and giving them the ability to regularly interact with customers. Almost all social media websites are free to join. While there may be a small fee for the business accounts, they do include more resources to help businesses track customer interactions and trends on their homepages. Social media marketing could potentially cost anywhere from $4,000 to $7,000 a month. This may seem like a lot of money for such small posts, but compared to the cost of traditional marketing and the time spent on physical marketing materials, the benefits of social media marketing greatly outweigh that cost. When you take that into consideration, this means that the big businesses that are paying people to produce social media advertisements are still saving a substantial amount of money by advertising online rather than in print or on television. Any way a company can save money on marketing will always be considered a pro in the business world.

The next pro on the list is the reach of the audience. Social media markets are constantly expanding, and every time someone follows a new account or adds a friend online, a new branch is created on the internet. The reach of social media is more than most people might realize. Instagram has 77.6 million users and is constantly growing. As the reach continues to grow, it becomes possible for people to share posts from the website via text messages, emails, or even direct messages on the app itself. The reach of marketing is endless if you utilize the right people to help you spread your message.

Social media is instant. With the advent of social media, people no longer have to wait for companies to mail out press releases or send out mass emails. One post can be shared with millions within seconds and will stay posted on the company page for all to see if they need to refer to it or find it again. The ability to communicate with customers and followers has allowed businesses to become more personable and customer service oriented than they were before. Communication channels are more open and the ability to answer the questions and concerns of multiple people at once has become easier than ever. It also serves to create a direct, two-way interaction between businesses and people. There isn't a huge divide between big business and the customer now as more businesses are responding directly to customers on their social media pages and creating more brand loyalty by interacting with their followers.

Social media has made research and feedback easy. Social media is a business that is always open, which means that you can get instant feedback on your marketing campaigns. This allows you to update and fix any small problems with your products or services from the feedback that you are getting from people. You might not like all of the feedback from customers, but it will be beneficial in the long run. You are able to reevaluate and update your campaign if something isn't working. Social media has an edit feature, which you don't have when you put something into physical print. And yes, people have already seen the post, but that doesn't mean you can't make some changes and send it out again. While some may consider this a pro, it can also be a con. Feedback is instant, and while you hope for entirely good feedback, it won't all be. There will always be someone that has a problem with your company and wants to complain about it on a public forum. That is just the way of the world. Some people are never satisfied. It is important to note, though, that even negative comments can be used to your advantage online. You may not have come up with a perfect solution for the individual who originally posted, but the effort that you put in will still be displayed, and other customers and reviewers will notice the time and effort that was taken to resolve the situation. Feedback is important to customers because it gives them a better sense of the company's intentions when they release new products to market. Are they just trying to sell another product, or are they listening to what we have been saying? Will the issues from the previous versions be fixed with this new release? The reason that we see constant updates and improvements of products and applications is because of the reviewers and testers that let the company know that something isn't working. It's more than likely that you have seen a mobile phone game advertised on Instagram at some point or another. If you take a moment to scroll through the comments on that feed, you might notice a lot of complaints about bugs in the system or people commenting about the level that they reached and the excitement that the game brings them. While the game producer may reply to some of the positive posts, they are paying close attention to the negative ones and the comments that get likes on them, symbolizing that others agree with that statement. It creates a way for the company to get the feedback needed in order to improve their product and keep people involved with it.

The last pro may be one of the biggest and most important. Social media is easily tracked. There are loads of software and analytic systems out there that can show you when your customers are online and what they are looking at more frequently. It gives you a better understanding of what posts they like the most, and which ones could use some improvement. It also lets you set a schedule of when to post in order to reach more people at the most active times.

Then, there are the cons.

Perhaps social media's largest con is that it's time-consuming. *Very* time-consuming. There are programs out there that you can use to schedule posts and plan in advance, but there is no way to schedule customer interaction. The internet is 24/7 and someone is always awake. While neither you nor your company need to be awake all day or night, there needs to be someone prepared to handle the havoc in the morning. Like we mentioned earlier, feedback is immediate, and while some people won't see them right away, comments that are left on posts need to be addressed, especially if they are shining a negative light on the product. Someone needs to manually sift through the comments, watch what people are posting, and tag the company in in order to deal with any customer service issues that may arise. This also shows customer interaction in general. Having a social media team is essential to the success of posting online. It is best to have one person to post and one to respond at minimum to make sure the bases are getting covered.

The next con on the list is negativity. While this may seem obvious, people on social media can be very hateful. There is no way to filter out hate comments or liars, and they just have to be addressed quickly and properly. The biggest lesson to know before entering the social media world is that, no matter how much customer service you provide, there will always be someone who reacts negatively. It's especially easy for people to be negative online because they aren't dealing with you face to face. Every company typically has a way to deal with negative users and try to resolve problems for them, but you can't expect everyone to be pleased with the results. Eventually, you have to move on towards other solutions.

This con can also be considered a pro depending on how you look at it. Social media is constantly changing. On the downside, about the time you get comfortable with the way something is performing and being used, it's going to change. Like everything else on the Internet, social media evolves as everyone's needs change. The positive side is that, as it changes, you can change with it. The basics of internet marketing are still going to apply with whatever changes are made.

The next big con on the list is that whatever is posted on the Internet stays there. While, you can make changes and updates to your posts online, you cannot stop people from sharing, screenshotting, commenting on, and reposting your original message. Before you post anything to your page, make sure that it is ready to be sent into the online world.

With posts being more casual and easily posted online, it can be hard to keep up with the constant conversations that are taking place. You don't want to leave one of your posts up to the interpretation of others, which is why you need to be clear and concise with anything you share online. Read it and re-read it, and even have a co-worker or two read it before you publish it. This will save you some time and hassle of having to try and fix any mistakes.

Now, let's discuss ROI (Return on Investment). ROI is difficult to measure.

If you are given the right tools to analyze ROI you should be able to measure it effectively as it relates to social media. You can then tell what is working and what isn't in order to improve your sales and link them back to the online platform. Businesses have social media platforms designed to track people's actions on their page but the problem with this is that it isn't always exact when it comes to sales, and it can't always be proven. If someone sees your Instagram post about the 20% off sale happening from Friday through Monday, but you also have that same message posted on your website and in an email that was sent out to all previous purchasers, there is no exact way to tell where that shopper came from. You could utilize an optional survey at the end of a purchase, or use promo codes to try and track where people saw the information. Otherwise, it will be a difficult measurement to get.

Is It Worth It?

The short answer is a resounding yes! There is no world in the future where Internet marketing and social media platforms will fail. While it is true that different platforms may come and go, their evolution will remain the same. Adaptation to new programs and settings may take some getting used to, but so does every new business marketing strategy out there. If your company is trying to get away with not building its social media presence, then you should deeply reconsider this. The rise of social media isn't going to be a passing trend, and with more and more people turning to Instagram and LinkedIn for connections in both the business and personal world, sales and marketing need to follow suit.

There are pros and cons to having a social media account, and there are a hundred different factors that can affect each one, but social media and Internet marketing are only going to grow as we move into the coming years. When you look at the big picture as far as marketing and sales go, Instagram has helped create more profit for businesses. Social media has created a gateway between customers and businesses where communication is key. People like interacting with other people. Seeing responses and hearing from businesses as they address problems will make customers feel more comfortable buying from them and returning to make more purchases.

The end goal of marketing online is to have customers return to your business and have them promote your company by word of mouth. They may be actually talking about the company or spreading the news online. You want customers to be excited to share your products with their social media family and to spread the word of their experience with your business. As discussed earlier in the book, brand advocates are on your side. Having people who speak on behalf of your company online is the goal. If you can get to the point where you have brand advocates and ambassadors sharing your product, then you will see online results. It won't be immediate and it will be time-consuming, but your company will be able to build its online brand and create a reputation for itself on social media.

Building a following, getting people to share pictures of their products, and discovering what's trending are all tasks that need to be worked on and accomplished every day for the social media team. There needs to be dedicated response times for customers and times where promotions are being put out. There are also a lot of little steps in between that have to be handled as well. While social media is difficult, especially when you are trying to work and manage multiple platforms at the same time, it's going to be the future of all marketing. Slowly, all print will fade and online shopping will become the majority of where sales develop. Be ready to accept the change of social media development. Learn how to improve your online business as you market to different crowds and people around the world.

Conclusion

Instagram marketing is taking the internet by storm. It is becoming more common and more popular among businesses. The general population of online users on Instagram has become more receptive to seeing advertisements, and they are a generation that shops and buys online. Instagram, along with other social media business accounts, has given companies the ability to determine what their customers are looking for. Analytics are readily available for businesses to review and study up on what is working and what isn't so that they can improve their online standing. Maybe you don't fully understand them right now, but you can learn all about how to use them to your company's advantage in order to better perform online. By studying the different analytics, you will have a better chance of gaining the attention that you need on your business page to drive the success of social media.

It's also not a bad idea to start with one social media page. Instagram is a great place to start because it offers most features from other applications while having one of the largest and most diverse audiences online. Starting with Instagram will allow your company to get an understanding of what works and what needs improvement along the way before you invest money into a scheduler service or hire a social media team. You want your page to be worth the time spent on it when it comes to bringing in customers. If it isn't working for you, then you need to seek a different solution as to how to gear your social media in the right direction.

Posting online has become the newest form of advertising. Even though people are shopping online, which works out in favor of the company, they are also sharing their new items and experiences online through photos and videos of themselves. Whenever a girl posts a selfie online and tags it with #feelingcute, she is sharing a piece of merchandise from the company or a makeup trend that she has been following recently. It all falls back into the product sale of what is being advertised online and marketed to the main pages. Whatever tags you add to a post will start to appear more often in your feed. While you probably won't notice it right away, if you start paying attention to what you are viewing on the platform, you will notice that it is tracking the images you like and people you follow in order to promote similar content to you as well.

Marketing has become as simple as posting at the right times and working with the right people to get your message across. Ambassadors are helping companies develop a following by promoting their brand and products to their followers. Those followers are watching their online idols show them new products and introduce them to businesses they haven't heard of before, but now they will want to shop at them.

Instagram alone has allowed people to create online shops and multiple highlight reels to post topic-specific photos and videos into categories. It's making it easier for people to find what they are looking for and to search through trending topics using hashtags and popular phrases. While it's easy enough to search for people online, most Instagrammers are searching through hashtag topics to find things that are relevant and that interest them.

We are entering into a world where technology is our main resource for practically everything, from communication to shopping and data collection. It shouldn't be surprising to find that marketing and sales are turning to advertisements online in the process to build up brand awareness of their company and products. Online marketing has made it easier for companies to communicate with their customers about different events and business information, and put out promotions at a more rapid rate. As we move further into the age of online communication and social media networking, there is more of a need to be able to produce online content and keep users engaged and responsive to online marketing tactics. Companies need to be ready to change and expand as the internet market grows. New social media companies will rise while others may fall. As long as your company is ready to jump onto the next trending site, there shouldn't be any problems with your online marketing strategies.

The internet is becoming the main way for businesses to grow and reach a larger range of people from different groups and backgrounds all around the world. As you develop new business strategies and marketing plans, make sure to include your business hashtags and continue to learn how to use #InstagramMarketing to your advantage.

References

Amed, I. (2015, August 23). How Do You Create Brand Awareness? Retrieved from https://www.businessoffashion.com/articles/basics/how-do-you-create-brand-awareness

Barker, S. (2018, March 26). 7 Simple Ways to Drive Sales on Social Media [With Examples]. Retrieved from https://medium.com/strategic-content-marketing/7-simple-ways-to-drive-sales-on-social-media-with-examples-8012193aa2fb

Cartwright, B. (2018, July 16). How to Run an Instagram Contest: A 10-Step Guide. Retrieved from https://blog.hubspot.com/marketing/instagram-contest-guide

Cooper, P. (2019, April 16). How the Instagram Algorithm Works in 2019 (And How to Work With It). Retrieved from https://blog.hootsuite.com/instagram-algorithm/

Decker, A. (2018, August 6). The Ultimate Guide to Brand Awareness. Retrieved from https://blog.hubspot.com/marketing/brand-awareness

DePhillips, K. (2015). 18 Reasons Why Social Media Marketing Is Important For Any Business. Retrieved from https://www.contentfac.com/9-reasons-social-media-marketing-should-top-your-to-do-list/

Errington, K. (2018, September 21). Social Media Pros and Cons: The Top 10. Retrieved from https://www.equinetmedia.com/blog/top-10-social-media-pros-and-cons

Gotter, A. (2019, April 14). Instagram Marketing: The Definitive Guide for Beginners. Retrieved from https://www.shopify.com/blog/instagram-marketing

Gregorio, J. (2014, June 11). The Pros and Cons of Social Media Marketing for Business. Retrieved from https://digitalmarketingphilippines.com/the-pros-and-cons-of-social-media-marketing-for-business/

Influencer Marketing Hub. (2019, June 13). The Beginner's Guide to Influencer Marketing on Instagram. Retrieved from https://influencermarketinghub.com/the-beginners-guide-to-influencer-marketing-on-instagram/

Later. (n.d.). Instagram Marketing: The Definitive Guide (2019). Retrieved from https://later.com/instagram-marketing/

Lowry, B. (2013, November 25). 6 Image Qualities Which May Drive More Likes on Instagram. Retrieved from https://www.curalate.com/blog/6-image-qualities-that-drive-more-instagram-likes/

Nelson, S. (2018, February 6). 7 reasons why social media marketing is important for your business. Retrieved from https://www.digitaldoughnut.com/articles/2018/february/7-reasons-why-social-media-marketing-is-important

Web Solutions of America. (2018, January 12). The Future of Online Marketing. Retrieved from https://www.wsoaonline.com/the-future-of-online-marketing/